WESAK

by Lisa J. Amstutz

PEBBLE
a capstone imprint

Published by Pebble, an imprint of Capstone
1710 Roe Crest Drive, North Mankato, Minnesota 56003
capstonepub.com

Library of Congress Cataloging-in-Publication Data is available on the Library of Congress website.

ISBN: 9780756576905 (hardcover)
ISBN: 9780756576967 (paperback)
ISBN: 9780756576974 (ebook PDF)

Summary: Wesak is about celebrating the Buddha. It is a Buddhist holiday. People clean and decorate temples for the celebration. Then, they honor the Buddha by making offerings and reciting holy texts. People also do good deeds during Wesak. Discover how people around the world celebrate this festive holiday.

Editorial Credits
Editor: Ericka Smith; Designer: Kayla Rossow; Media Researcher: Svetlana Zhurkin; Production Specialist: Katy LaVigne

Image Credits
Alamy: Godong, 7, World Religions Photo Library, 9; Dreamstime: DiegoFiore, 25, Jackhor Meng Siang, 20, Liphin Ho, 5; Getty Images: Akarawut Lohacharoenvanich, 12, Andrea Pistolesi, 29, Bayu Wisnu Wardhana, 15, Sunphol Sorakul, 23; Shutterstock: AhXiong, 17, Bangkok Click Studio, 21, Calvin Chan, 27, Emma manners, 13, Heng Lim, 18, Huy Thoai, 19, IceBerg10, 10, Panu Kosonen, 1, Panwasin seemala, 14, Rafal Kulik (background), back cover and throughout, Titima Ongkantong, 11, Uditha Wickramanayaka, cover, Vietnam Stock Images, 28

All internet sites appearing in back matter were available and accurate when this book was sent to press.

Printed and bound in China. 5593

TABLE OF CONTENTS

Words in **bold** are in the glossary.

WHAT IS WESAK?

Lanterns sparkle. **Chants** ring out. Wesak is here! It is time to go to the **temple**.

Wesak is a Buddhist festival. Many people in Asia celebrate this holiday. People dance, make music, and share food. The celebration can last for days. It is a bright and happy time.

Wesak is a holy day too. It is a time to worship and learn. It is also a time to think of others.

Wesak is also called Vesak or Buddha Day. It honors the Buddha's birth. Some remember his death and **enlightenment** on this day too.

The Buddha was born around 563 BCE in India. His name was Siddhartha Gautama.

Gautama grew up as a prince. His life was easy and safe. When he was 29 years old, he went out into the streets. There he saw an old man, a sick man, and a dead man. He was sad to see people suffer. Then he saw a **monk**. The monk was at peace. How could this be?

Gautama sees an old man.

Gautama had to find out. He gave up his riches. He left home and became a holy man. He tried to find meaning in life. He **fasted** and **meditated**.

One day Gautama sat under a tree. He focused his mind. He found wisdom and love. His mind was at peace.

Gautama began to teach people what he had learned about suffering and how to get away from it. He became known as the Buddha. This means "the enlightened one." Many people followed him.

Now, about 500 million people are Buddhists. Most live in Asia.

The Buddha teaching followers

A family praying in front of a Buddha statue

WHEN IS WESAK?

In most places, the date of Wesak changes each year. Wesak follows a **lunar** calendar. The holiday takes place during the fourth month when there's a full moon. That usually happens between April and June.

In Japan, the date of Wesak does not change. It is always April 8.

Buddhists in Japan visit temples on April 8.

WHERE IS WESAK CELEBRATED?

Buddhists all over the world celebrate Wesak. Each area has its own traditions.

In South Korea, there is a Lotus Lantern Festival. Paper lanterns drape temple walls, and people serve food and tea.

South Korea

In Malaysia, monks place a huge painting in the sun on big posts. It is called a *thangka*. People run under it. They hope this will bring them blessings.

In Indonesia, people light lanterns. Then they let them go. The lights float into the night sky.

Indonesia

GETTING READY

When it's almost time for Wesak, many people go to the temple to prepare. They clean the temple. They hang flags and lanterns. They decorate with flowers.

People clean their homes and streets too. They put up lights.

A temple decorated for Wesak

WESAK IS HERE!

As dawn breaks, people head to the temple. Some will stay there all day and night. Many wear white clothes. They bring candles, flowers, and food. They burn **incense**.

People lighting incense during Wesak

Buddhist monks at a temple

At the temple, people do things
to honor the Buddha for his life and
teachings. They make offerings to
statues of the Buddha. They chant.
This helps them clear their minds. They
think about what the Buddha taught.
Monks recite **sutras**, or holy texts.

A statue sits at the front of the temple. People come to bathe the Buddha. They pour water or sweet tea over its shoulders. As they pour, they think. They clear their minds of hate and greed.

Bathing the Buddha

At home, people may worship by a **shrine**. It holds a statue or image of the Buddha. The family gives offerings of flowers or fruit. They burn candles and incense.

Wesak is a time to be kind to other people. People do good deeds. They give to the temple and to those in need. Some give blood during this time. Others give out free food in the streets. These acts remind them of the Buddha's kindness.

Wesak is a day of kindness to animals too. Many people do not eat meat during this time. They may eat a meal of rice in milk. This is a meal the Buddha once ate.

In some parts of the world, people buy caged birds or other animals. They set them free. But tame animals may not be able to find food on their own, so many people have stopped doing this.

A women offering the Buddha rice and milk

Crowds line the streets to watch Wesak parades. Flowers and sparkling lights decorate floats. They show scenes from the Buddha's life. **Pandols** tell stories about the Buddha too. These large pictures flash and glow.

People parade with flags and lanterns. They chant and dance. Some people do the "three steps, one bow" **ritual**. They take three steps and bow. Then they repeat those actions. They pray for peace and blessings.

A Wesak parade

As night falls, candles glow. People sing and chant late into the night. They gather near statues of the Buddha. They hold candles.

Then Wesak comes to an end—until next year!

GLOSSARY

chant (CHANT)—to say or sing a phrase over and over

enlightenment (en-LITE-en-muhnt)—knowledge or understanding

fast (FAST)—to give up eating for a period of time

incense (IN-sens)—a substance that makes a sweet odor when burned

lunar (LOO-nuhr)—having to do with the moon

meditate (MED-i-tayt)—to think deeply and quietly

monk (MUHNGK)—a man who lives in a religious community and promises to devote his life to his religion

pandol (PAN-dahl)—an illustration with lights

ritual (RICH-ew-uhl)—an act performed as part of a ceremony

shrine (SHRINE)—a place used for religious celebrations

sutra (SOO-truh)—a holy text in Buddhism

temple (TEM-puhl)—a building used for worship

READ MORE

Bradley, Fleur. *My Life as a Buddhist*. Ann Arbor, MI: Cherry Lake Publishing, 2022.

Brennan, Katy. *Buddhism*. New York: Britannica Educational Publishing, 2018.

Mansfield, Nicole A. *Easter*. North Mankato, MN: Capstone, 2024.

INTERNET SITES

Kiddle: Vesak Facts for Kids
kids.kiddle.co/Vesak

Multicultural Kid Blogs: 10 Fun Facts for Kids About Vesak
multiculturalkidblogs.com/2019/05/17/10-fun-facts-vesak-2

YouTube (Behind the News): What Is the Vesak Festival & What Does It Mean to Buddhists?
youtube.com/watch?v=U1pQwj-CNZ8

INDEX

ABOUT THE AUTHOR

Lisa J. Amstutz is the author of more than 150 children's books on topics ranging from applesauce to zebra mussels. An ecologist by training, she enjoys sharing her love of nature with kids. Lisa lives on a small farm with her family.